Kenya

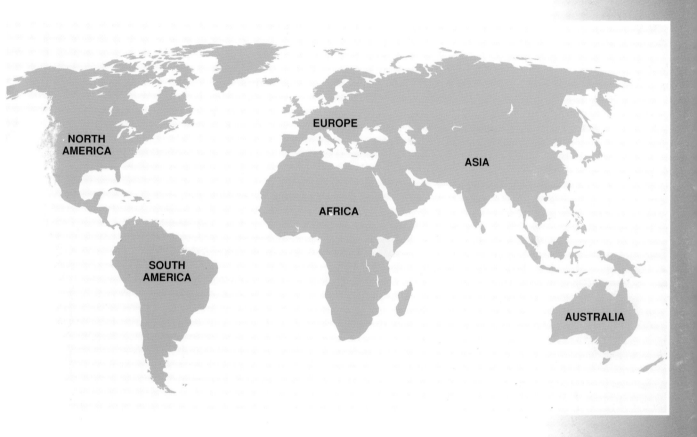

Fred Martin

Heinemann
LIBRARY

First published in Great Britain by Heinemann Library
Halley Court, Jordan Hill, Oxford OX2 8EJ
a division of Reed Educational and Professional Publishing Ltd

Heinemann is a registered trademark of Reed Educational and Professional Publishing Ltd

OXFORD FLORENCE PRAGUE MADRID ATHENS
MELBOURNE AUCKLAND KUALA LUMPUR SINGAPORE TOKYO
IBADAN NAIROBI KAMPALA JOHANNESBURG GABORONE
PORTSMOUTH NH (USA) CHICAGO MEXICO CITY SAO PAULO

Designed by AMR
Illustrations by Art Construction
Printed in Hong Kong / China

03 02 01 00 99
10 9 8 7 6 5 4 3 2 1

ISBN 0 431 04555 0

British Library Cataloguing in Publication Data

Martin, Fred, 1948-
Step into Kenya
1. Kenya – Geography – Juvenile literature
I.Title II.Kenya
916.7'62

This title is also available in a hardback edition (ISBN 0 431 04554 2).

Acknowledgements
The Publishers would like to thank the following for permission to reproduce photographs:
Aspect Pictures, Peter Carmichael, p.23, Tom Nebbia, p.8; Hutchison Library, Timothy Beddow p.25; Link Picture Library, Sue Carpenter, p.19; Panos Pictures, Jeremy Hartley, pp.4, 26, Betty Press, pp.5, 24, 29, Sean Sprague, p.14; Planet Earth Pictures, Sean Avery, p.6, Roger de la Harpe, p.10; Still Pictures, Adrian Arib, pp.18, 28, M&C Denis-Huot, p.9, Mark Edwards, pp.11, 22, Fritz Polking, p.7, Hartmut Schwarzbach, p.15; Trip Photo Library, p.12, 13, 16, 17, 20, 21, D. Saunders, p.27.

Cover photographs: J. Allan Cash and Robert Harding Picture Library

Our thanks to Betty Root for her comments in the preparation of this book.

Every effort has been made to contact holders of any material reproduced in this book. Any omissions will be rectified in subsequent printings if notice is given to the Publisher.

CONTENTS

INTRODUCTION TO KENYA

Kenya: towns and population

KENYA'S MOUNTAIN

Kenya is a country in Africa. It gets its name from Mount Kenya which means 'mountain of whiteness'. This is because there is always snow on the top. Mount Kenya is on the **equator**.

City Population

- ○ Over 1,000,000
- ◔ Over 100,000
- ◑ Under 100,000
- ● Capital

0   100 km

SUDAN

ETHIOPIA

Lake Turkana

UGANDA

N

KENYA

SOMALIA

● Kitale

● Eldoret

Kisumu   Nanyuki ●   Mt Kenya ▲

Equator 0°

Lake Victoria   Kericho ● Nakuru ● Nyeri ●

● Thika

Nairobi ●

Malindi ○

TANZANIA   Mombasa ◑

INDIAN OCEAN

35° E   40° E

These schoolgirls are waving Kenya's flag. This is to celebrate Kenya's Independence Day.

KENYA'S PEOPLE

For several hundred years, people moved to Kenya from other parts of Africa. The Kikuyu and the Maasai tribes are two of these groups of people. Their land was taken over by Britain about 150 years ago.

Many people in Kenya get their water from a village well or pump.

A NEW COUNTRY

In 1963, Kenya became a new country with its own rulers and **government**. Kenya's flag has a shield and two spears. The country's colours are green, yellow and black.

About 28 million people live in Kenya. The country's **population** is growing very quickly. Most Kenyan people are poor compared to most people in rich countries like the UK or Australia.

Some scientists think that the first humans lived in Africa. Old bones belonging to these people have been found in Kenya.

THE LAND

Kenya: natural features

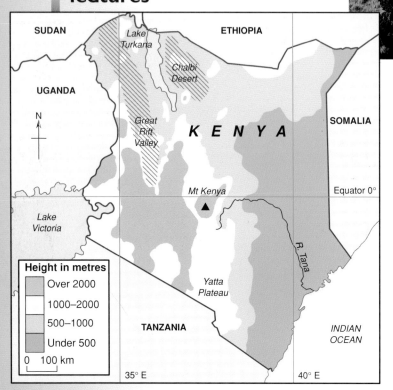

Mount Kenya is 5199 metres high. This is about five times higher than Britain's highest mountain.

HILLS AND MOUNTAINS

Mount Kenya is the highest mountain in Kenya. There are more hills and mountains in the south and west of Kenya. Some of the mountains are **volcanoes**. Mount Kenya does not **erupt** any more so it is an extinct volcano. Others still do erupt. They are active. There are lakes in the **craters** of some old volcanoes.

THE GREAT RIFT

There is a giant crack in the rocks across Kenya. The crack is called a rift. The crack makes a long and deep valley with very steep sides. It is called the Great Rift Valley.

THE PLAINS

The land is lower and flatter in the east and north of Kenya than in the south and west. These low, flat areas are called plains. Most rivers on the plains only flow for part of the year. This is because it does not rain for several months.

Lake Victoria is the world's biggest freshwater lake. Only part of Lake Victoria is in Kenya.

The River Mara flows through an area of flat plains. Trees only grow close together where it is wet near the river.

7

WEATHER, PLANTS AND ANIMALS

WEATHER

The **equator** passes through Kenya. The weather is usually very hot near the equator, but Kenya is different. It is cooler because the land is high up.

There are two seasons in Kenya. One is hot and wet. The other is warm and dry. The north is almost dry enough to be a desert. Sometimes no rain falls for several months. This is called a drought.

This is a **savanna** landscape. It has grass and scattered trees. There are some clouds but it does not rain very often. The animals are called impala.

There are about 1.3 million wildebeest in Kenya's Maasai Mara National Park.

PLANTS

Most of the land in Kenya has grass with some trees called savanna **vegetation**. The grass grows tall after it rains. It turns brown and dies down when it becomes dry and hot.

WILDLIFE

In Kenya, there are herds of wildebeest, zebra, gazelle and elephants. The 'big cats' are lions and cheetahs. Crocodiles and hippos live in the rivers. Many of the animals live in **game reserves** and **national parks**.

The animals crossing the river are wildebeest. These animals roam wild in the grassland areas. The odd one out is a zebra.

VILLAGES AND CITIES

VILLAGE PEOPLE

Most people in Kenya live in villages in the countryside. Only one quarter of them live in towns or cities. Whole families live together in a group of round huts. This is called a *manyatta*. Children, parents and grandparents live together. Sometimes aunts and uncles live with them.

THE CAPITAL CITY

Kenya's capital city is Nairobi. There are offices, shops, blocks of flats and houses in Nairobi.

This village woman is making a house using wood, mud and straw. She is putting cattle dung on the roof to keep the rain out.

Some poor people build their own homes in Nairobi. They use scrap wood and other things they can find to make them. These groups of poor housing are called shanty towns. Rich people have better houses.

MOVING HOUSE

Camel and cattle herders in the north of Kenya move their herds from place to place to find water and fresh grass. These people are called nomads. They take their houses with them when they move. The houses are made from wood, leather and straw. This makes them light and easy to take apart and carry.

The city of Nairobi will be 100 years old in 1999. Before 1899, there was nothing there except a watering hole where Maasai farmers brought their cattle to drink.

A CITY FAMILY

LIVING IN MACHAKOS

Mr Muunda Mutisia is married to Jennifer Muunda. They have two children called Mike and Samuel. They live in a housing estate in the town of Machakos.

Samuel and his parents outside their home.

Their house is made from bricks. It has a tiled roof and a concrete floor. The family grow vegetables in their garden.

This is the living room in the family home.

A maid cooks meals on a gas cooker and a stove that burns oil.

WORK AND SCHOOL

Muunda and Jennifer both work in Nairobi. He works in an office. She sells **craft goods** in Nairobi City Market.

Mike goes to a secondary school. Samuel is in his last year in primary school. There are almost 50 children in some of the classes. They have to pass exams to get a place in a secondary school. The children and their father like to play football. Jennifer goes to keep-fit classes.

Muunda at work in his office.

Jennifer has a shop where she sells masks and carvings of animals.

FARMING IN KENYA

ANIMAL HERDERS

Some farmers have herds of cattle, sheep or goats. This is called pastoral farming. These farmers use the animals' meat and milk for food. The skins are used to make clothes and houses. Most animal herders keep moving their herds to find new grazing land and water.

Maasai people keep herds of cattle. The cattle give them meat, milk and leather.

GROWING CROPS

In Kenya, farmers grow **grain crops** such as maize and millet. This is called **arable** farming. They also grow vegetables and bananas.

FARMS IN KENYA

Most crops are grown on small farms called *shambas*. The farm work is done by hand instead of by machines. Most of the food grown on the *shamba* is eaten by the family. The rest is sold in markets. Some farmers grow tea or sugar cane to sell to factories. The biggest farms are called **estates**. They grow only one crop, such as coffee, tea, sugar cane or flowers. These are sold to other countries.

Men look after the animals in Kenya. Women grow the crops.

Tea pickers pick tea leaves on an estate. The tea is sold to countries where it is too cold to grow tea.

LIVING IN THE COUNTRY

VERONICA'S FAMILY

Veronica Wangari Kamande and her seven children live in a Mangu village in Kenya. Veronica works as a cleaner and cook in a school.

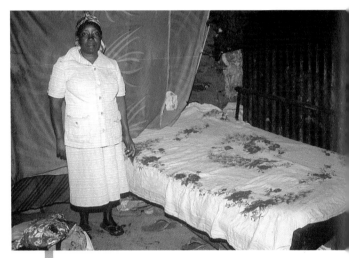

Veronica by her bed inside her house.

THE FAMILY'S HOME

The family lives in a house made from **corrugated iron**. The floor is bare ground. There is only one room in the house. The family eat, sleep, work and cook in this room. There is only one fresh water tap in the village. There is no electricity.

Patrick aged ten is lighting the fire to do the cooking. The house gets very smoky.

A classroom in the village primary school.

The village tap.

THE VILLAGE PRIMARY SCHOOL

Veronica's youngest children, Patrick and John, go to a village primary school. The classrooms do not have doors or windows. Veronica has to pay a **school fee** every term. It is very hard to earn enough money to pay the fee.

Patrick, John and a young friend with their pet rabbits.

MARKETS AND SHOPS

MARKET DAYS

People in the country do most of their buying and selling in street markets. Village women walk to the market carrying food from their family farms. They sit on the ground under the shade of an umbrella and sell the food.

FACTORY GOODS

Everything people needed used to be grown or made by village **craftspeople**. They made pots, tools and strips of cloth. Now people buy goods made in factories.

Most people buy their food in street markets.

A small shop selling women's and children's clothes in Nairobi.

SMALL SHOPS

There are many small shops in Kenya. The shops are full of tins and packets. Most people don't have fridges. Tins and packets are the only ways of keeping food. Many different types of goods are brought in from other countries.

CITY SHOPS

The biggest shops are in Nairobi and Mombasa. The richest people shop in department stores and shopping malls.

Many people in the shanty towns grow their own food. This is what they did when they lived in villages.

KENYAN FOOD

A plot of land where a family grows most of its own food. Bananas are growing here.

COUNTRY COOKING

Maize is one of the main foods in Kenya. Cassava, millet, and green bananas are other basic foods. The Somali people collect and eat wild honey.

FOOD FROM ANIMALS

Animal herders get milk and sometimes blood from their animals. The blood is rich in iron and vitamins. The people mix it with their food. Animals are only killed for their meat when they are old.

COOKING PROBLEMS

Cooking in Kenya is never quick or easy. Sticks have to be collected for firewood. Water has to be carried from a well or stream. People have to make their own flour from grain. Farmers have to store food from their harvest in bins made from mud and straw. But insects and animals bite through the bins and eat the food.

Some tourist hotels in Kenya's game parks offer a meal of buffalo steak.

Meals are cooked inside on wood fires or on simple cookers that burn oil.

MADE IN KENYA

VILLAGE CRAFTS

There are not many factories in Kenya. People often make what they need. They build their own homes, make pots, farm tools, clothes, musical instruments and ornaments. They learn these skills from their parents.

USING SCRAP

In the cities, people make things in small workshops or in the open air. They use scrap materials to make and repair metal goods, furniture and almost anything else.

These workers in Nairobi are making things from metal. They work outside.

Cloth with colourful prints is made in factories.

FACTORIES

Some goods are made in factories. A crop called sisal is made into rope. Sugar cane is made into sugar and coffee beans are made into coffee. Cement is made to help make roads and new buildings. **Crude oil** from other countries is refined in Mombasa.

CHANGE

Kenya is one of the world's poorest countries. One reason is that it does not have many factory goods to sell to other countries.

Only seven out of every 100 people in Kenya work in factories.

GETTING AROUND

GOING ON FOOT

People in Kenya are used to walking. They walk to fetch firewood or water, to look after animals or to go to school. Some people walk for several hours every day.

OFF-ROAD

Some roads between towns have hard surfaces. But many roads and tracks in the countryside are too rough to be used by cars. Roads are sometimes washed away by heavy rain. The only way to travel is to use a Land Rover or another type of 'off-road' vehicle.

Many people in Nairobi catch a minivan called a *matatus* to get about. They can get very crowded.

TRAVEL IN THE CITY

In the cities there are more rich people and so more cars. But most people are poor and travel by bus.

LONG DISTANCE

There are not many train services. One line links Mombasa and Nairobi. The journey takes about fourteen hours travelling at about 35 km per hour. There is a one-hour air flight, but it is much more expensive.

The main bus station in Nairobi is called 'Machakos airport' as a joke. Buses go in all directions from the bus station.

This train travels between the cities of Nairobi and Mombasa. There are not many railway lines in Kenya.

SPORTS AND PLAY

Girls at school playing with a ball.

KENYAN RUNNERS

Athletes from Kenya often win races. They have won gold medals in many international competitions. Kenyan runners are best at middle and long distance races.

GROWING SPORTS

Some people play sports, such as football and basketball. Teams from Kenya take part in international competitions. One of the world's toughest car races is the East African Safari Rally. People can watch the rally as it goes through Kenya.

VILLAGE PLAY

Children in Kenya like ball games and games of tag. They play team sports when they are in school. They also take part in dancing and singing during festivals.

TOURISTS

Many tourists visit Kenya. Some go to the beaches on the east coast. Others go to see the animals in the **game reserves**.

Henry Rono is one of Kenya's most successful runners. In 1978, he broke five world records in only 50 days.

Tourists go to Kenya to see the wildlife. Game reserves are special areas where wildlife is protected.

CUSTOMS AND FESTIVALS

Children often have the job of looking after some farm animals.

GETTING MARRIED

Every tribe in Kenya has its own local festivals and customs. These are to do with farming, their religion or events such as marriage. One marriage custom is that the groom's family gives a gift for a wife. The usual gift is five cattle or sixty goats. People show how rich they are by the number of animals they own.

GROWING OLDER

There are ceremonies to show when boys become warriors. In one ceremony, a boy's mother shaves his head. When they are older, boys become **elders**. There are also ceremonies to show when girls become women.

Maasai men dance by leaping high in the air.

DANCING

The Maasai tribe have one unusual type of dance. The men leap high into the air to show how strong they are. Women are not allowed to do this. Dances are sometimes put on just for tourists. In the future, the real reason for the dances may be forgotten.

Kenyatta Day on 20 October is a special day for all Kenyans. Jomo Kenyatta was Kenya's first president. The day is to celebrate when Kenya became independent.

KENYA FACTFILE

People

People from Kenya are called Kenyans.

Capital city

The capital city of Kenya is Nairobi.

Largest cities

Nairobi is the largest city, with nearly one-and-a-half million people. The second largest city is Mombasa and Kisumu is the third largest city.

Head of country

Kenya is ruled by a president and a **government**. Jomo Kenyatta was the first president, after Kenya became **independent**.

Population

There are over 28 million people living in Kenya.

Money

The money in Kenya is called the Kenyan shilling (KSh).

Language

There are several languages spoken in Kenya. Many are local tribal languages. The most common are Kikuyu, Luo, Luyia, Kamba and Kalenjin. English is also spoken.

Religion

Most people in Kenya are Christian, but many have traditional African beliefs, and a few are Muslims.

GLOSSARY

arable growing crops

corrugated iron sheets of iron that are shaped to give a wavy surface

craft goods things that people have made themselves, to use or to sell

craftspeople people who make craft goods

crater a bowl-shaped area in the top of an extinct volcano

crude oil oil that has been taken out of the ground, before it is made into other things, such as petrol

elders older people in a tribe, who make decisions

equator the line around the middle of the earth

erupt when a volcano erupts, hot rocks and lava burst out of its top and roll down its sides

estates very large farms that are run as businesses

game reserve areas where wildlife is looked after and protected

government people who run a country

grain crops crops, such as wheat, that give grains that can be made into flour and other food products

independent a country with its own government

national parks large areas where the natural landscape and wildlife are protected

population the people who live in a country or area

protected looked after, nobody is allowed to hunt the animals or to harm the landscape

savanna where there is a hot and wet season and a warm and dry season

school fee money paid to a school, so that children can go there

vegetation trees and plants

volcano a mountain made from hot rock that bursts out through the earth's surface

INDEX